YOUR PLACE —IN— SPACE

a career guide for girls

BY ELIZABETH BRADSHAW

© Elizabeth A. Bradshaw 2021

ISBN 9780578955742

All rights reserved.

Forward

Astronauts, space explorers and trailblazers inspire us because they figure out the way forward, regardless of the obstacles, challenges and hardships. They are driven to solve a problem, find a new way or just motivated by the desire to explore the vastness of space and our planet earth. Their journeys of discovery and exploration are too frequently overlooked and not available to inspire girl's hopes, dreams and ambitions of space and the stars.

Elizabeth Bradshaw has addressed that challenge with her middle school book that tells the stories of female trailblazers and pioneers in the space industry. It is a book that I would have loved to have read on my path to being a Rocket Scientist, working on the Voyager 2 and Parker Solar Probe missions at NASA's Jet Propulsion Laboratory.

This book, *Your Place in Space*, is filled with engaging stories that are key to unlocking the potential of the rising generation of future scientists and engineers who are looking for information and inspiration in their quest to reach for the stars.

Sylvia Acevedo

Rocket Scientist, Former CEO of the Girl Scouts of the USA and Author of *Path to the Stars*

Author's Note

Who do you picture working in the space industry? Who do you think designs rockets, programs rovers, and ventures into outer space? What does a scientist, engineer, or programmer look like to you? Take a second, jot down some notes or a quick sketch.

If you are like most people, a scientist is a wild-haired, white-coated lab dweller. An engineer is a glasses-wearing nerd who works with machines. Computer programmers are, of course, the ultimate geeks, hiding behind their screens while designing computers, apps, and websites.

If you are like most people, you probably drew men. Back in the 1960s and 70s, just 1% of children pictured a woman when asked to draw a scientist. That number is rising but today, by age 12, over 70% of study participants still draw a male scientist.[1]

The space industry is one of the most vibrant, exciting, and fastest-evolving fields! Plans are underway to return to the moon and finally send humans to Mars. Private companies and new international space agencies are joining the world of space. Who works in this industry? Most people will think of astronauts, and some will consider astronomers or aerospace engineers. However, the space industry is so much broader. On the following pages, you will find 18 careers spanning the space industry. For each, I have included a description discussing what these professionals do, where they work, and what they study. You will also find a "career pioneer," a woman who paved the way and opened the doors to this field for women to come. Finally, you will find a biography of current female scientists, engineers, and other professionals pushing the boundaries of and excelling in their fields. I hope you will find their stories as inspiring as I do. Keep reading, keep studying, and keep exploring. Whatever your interests, there's a place in space for you.

Table of Contents

Aerospace Engineer	6
Astrobiologist	8
Astronaut	10
Astronomer & Astrophysicist	12
Atmospheric Scientist	14
Chemical Engineer	16
Chemist	18
Computer Scientist	20
Electrical Engineer	22
Geologist	24
Materials Engineer	26
Mechanical Engineer	28
Mission Controller	30
Physicist	32
Pilot	34
Planetary Scientist	36
Robotics Engineer	38
Space Medicine Specialist	40
Other Careers to Consider	42
Advice & Inspiration	44
Name Index	45
References	45
Acknowledgements	47

Four hundred thousand workers in countless fields collaborated to design, build, test, and apply every component of the Apollo program, including the massive Saturn V rocket.[2]

Aerospace Engineer

Related Careers: Electrical Engineer, Mechanical Engineer, Robotics Engineer

Aerospace engineers design, build, and test airplanes, rockets, spacecraft, and missiles. These engineers work with everything from airplanes to Mars rovers! There are two main branches of aerospace engineering: aeronautical and astronautical. Aeronautical engineers focus on airplanes and flight within Earth's atmosphere. Astronautical engineers design rockets plus spacecraft like rovers and satellites. Most aerospace engineers work with universities, government labs, or private companies. Engineers in this field must understand math, aerodynamics, materials science, software, physics, and more.

Aerospace engineers work with rockets as well as launch pads like Launch Complex 39 at Kennedy Space Center.

Career Pioneer: Mary Jackson

Mary Jackson (1921-2005) was the first female, African-American engineer at NASA. She started her career as a "computer," calculating orbits for the space program. In 1953, she began working with an engineer who suggested she complete an engineering training program. Although Jackson needed special permission to attend the segregated classes, she completed the program in 1958. Jackson worked as an aerospace engineer for 20 years.[3] **Left: Mary Jackson working at NASA**

Aerospace Engineer

Professional Profile: Dr. Heather Wiest

NAME: Heather Wiest

CAREER: Aerospace Engineer

EDUCATION:

- Bachelor's: Mechanical Engineering, Rose-Hulman Institute of Technology
- Master's: Aerospace Engineering, Purdue University
- Ph.D.: Aerospace Engineering, Purdue University

EMPLOYER: Blue Origin

TITLE: Mechanical Engineer III

"It is really exciting to be a part of commercial space as it rapidly grows."

Dr. Heather Wiest is an aerospace engineer at the Cape Canaveral Research Station. She specializes in launch pad design. She works with the system that transports helium to the launch pad. Working at Cape Canaveral, Dr. Wiest gets to watch rocket launches in the middle of the workday! She is also managing the construction of a new helium pipeline.

Dr. Wiest earned her Florida Professional Engineering (PE) license. In graduate school, she received research fellowships through the National Science Foundation and Zonta International. As a high school student, she was inspired by an engineering camp. At first, she had trouble deciding between aerospace and biomedical engineering, but ultimately chose mechanical engineering for its broader focus. She enjoys working with the Society of Women Engineers and at STEM outreach events. In her free time, she sails on the Banana River in Florida, which has great views of Kennedy Space Center.

Astrobiologist

Related Careers: Astronomer & Astrophysicist, Atmospheric Scientist, Planetary Scientist

Astrobiologists are a type of planetary scientist. They study planets and moons to explore the possibility of extraterrestrial life. Astrobiologists determine if planetary bodies might have the conditions to support life such as moderate temperatures and liquid water. They also work with astronomers to look for evidence of life. This is done with telescopes, landers, or rovers. Some astrobiology experiments are even done on the International Space Station! Most astrobiologists work in labs and universities. These scientists use chemistry, geology, computer modelling, and, of course, biology.

Exoplanets like Kepler 1649-c may host life. Astrobiologists help answer the ultimate question, "Are we alone?"

Career Pioneer: Rosalind Franklin

Rosalind Franklin (1920-1958) was a British biologist know for her work discovering the structure of DNA. Franklin earned a degree in physical chemistry from the University of Cambridge. At the Biophysical Laboratory, Franklin used a technique called X-ray diffraction to study DNA. She discovered the density of DNA and its spiral-like pattern. Later in her career, she also researched the structure of viruses.[4]

Left: Franklin in 1956.

Astrobiologist

Professional Profile: Julia Brodsky

NAME: Julia Brodsky

CAREER: Astrobiologist

EDUCATION:
- Bachelor's: Physics, St. Petersburg Polytechnic University (St. Petersburg, Russia)
- Master's: Space Science, St. Petersburg Polytechnic University

EMPLOYER: Blue Marble Space Institute of Science

TITLE: Affiliate Research Scientist

"Do not be shy to approach people and ask questions"

Julia Brodsky is an astrobiologist and science educator. In her words, astrobiology "presents a holistic view of the world, bringing together the sciences of cosmology, astronomy, physics, biology, geology and paleontology." She is the founder and lead instructor of a science education program. She began her career in the space industry as an avionics instructor for the crew of the International Space Station. She has also worked with climate satellites and the Orion program.

Ms. Brodsky is the recipient of the Silver Snoopy Award, presented by a NASA astronaut for outstanding work towards flight safety and mission success. She was inspired to pursue her current career by science fiction. In her free time, she enjoys poetry, rock climbing, and working with the homeschool community.

"My favorite aspect of this field is that it is all about the future"

Astronaut

Related Careers: Aerospace Engineer, Astronomer & Astrophysicist, Mission Controller

Astronauts are the explorers who have either been to space or who will travel to space. The term "astronaut" derives from the Greek words for "star sailor." Other space programs use names like "cosmonaut" to describe their crews. Astronaut selection is very competitive! Potential astronauts must have at least a master's degree in engineering, math, or science. Astronauts have to complete extensive training. Once assigned a flight, the astronauts train for their specific mission and, finally, fly into space! NASA has employed a total of over 300 astronauts, including more than 50 women.

The "Mercury 7" were the first American astronauts.

Career Pioneer: Valentina Tereshkova

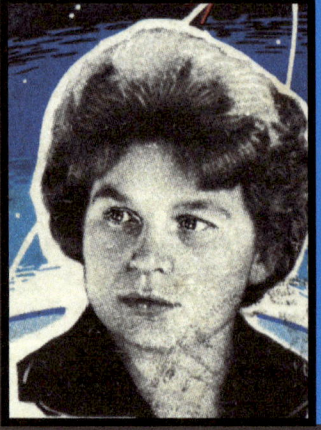

Valentina Tereshkova (1937-) was the first woman to fly in space. While working at a textile mill, Tereshkova began parachuting. In 1961, she wrote a letter volunteering to be a Soviet cosmonaut. She completed her training and was chosen for the Vostok 6 flight. On June 16, 1963, she launched into orbit and completed a 70-hour spaceflight. She safely returned to Earth and later became an engineer and parliament member.[5]

Left: Tereshkova on a 1963 Soviet postage stamp.

Astronaut

Professional Profile: Jasmin Moghbeli

NAME: Jasmin Moghbeli

CAREER: Pilot & Astronaut

EDUCATION:

- Bachelor's: Aerospace Engineering, Massachusetts Institute of Technology
- Master's: Aerospace Engineering, Naval Postgraduate School

EMPLOYER: NASA & the United States Marine Corps

TITLE: Astronaut

"I love the adventurous aspect of space exploration."

Major Jasmin Moghbeli is a NASA astronaut. She is a former Cobra helicopter and Marine Corps test pilot. Her specialty is evaluating new aircraft, spacecraft, and their subsystems. She ensures that these systems meet mission objectives and minimize human error. Currently, she works with the Human Landing System, developing the next generation of lunar landers. She "provides feedback on the designs of these systems from the operator's perspective." Major Moghbeli was selected to join NASA's Artemis team and is currently awaiting flight assignment.

She earned numerous recognitions in the military. These include four Air Medals and two Navy and Marine Corps Commendation Medals. She also earned three Navy and Marine Corps Achievement awards and several other honors. Major Moghbeli was inspired to become an astronaut when she wrote a sixth-grade book report about Valentina Tereshkova, the first woman in space. She enjoys stand-up paddle boarding and dancing.

Astronomer & Astrophysicist

Related Careers: Atmospheric Scientist, Physicist, Mission Controller

Astronomers study planets, stars, moons, galaxies, and other parts of outer space. Astrophysics is a field that combines parts of astronomy and physics. Astrophysicists study gravity, light, and the beginning of the universe. They use telescopes to study outer space objects, called celestial bodies. Some telescopes are Earth-based, while some, like the space-based Hubble Space Telescope, orbit the Earth. Most astronomers and astrophysicists have Ph.D.s and work at universities. These scientists use computer modelling, physics, math, and astronomy.

Astronomers study everything from the planets to the whole universe.

Career Pioneer: Vera Rubin

Vera Rubin (1928-2016) was an American astronomer known for her work with dark matter. Rubin grew up fascinated by astronomy and stargazing. She was the only astronomy student to graduate from her class at the all-female Vassar College. Her astronomical observations revealed that galaxies are mostly made of dark matter. Rubin was elected to the National Academy of Science and awarded the National Medal of Science in 1993.[6]

Left: Rubin in 2009

Astronomer & Astrophysicist

Professional Profile: Dr. Abby Vieregg

NAME: Abby Vieregg

CAREER: Astrophysicist

EDUCATION:
- Bachelor's: Physics, Dartmouth College
- Ph.D.: Physics, University of California Los Angeles

EMPLOYER: University of Chicago

TITLE: Associate Professor of Physics

"I get to work with people from all around the world to solve some really interesting problems and learn about the universe"

Dr. Abby Vieregg works in the field of experimental particle astrophysics and cosmology. She designs and builds telescopes that study the "extremely high-energy universe and the extremely early universe." One such telescope, ANITA, flies over Antarctica on a balloon. It searches for fundamental particles called neutrinos.

For her work, Dr. Vieregg received the Presidential Early Career Award for Scientists and Engineers and NASA's Roman Technology Fellowship. Dr. Vieregg has a lifelong love of math, science, and building with her hands. Her career allows her to do all of those things and share her passion with students.

"Keep asking questions, study math and science, and find what delights you."

Atmospheric Scientist

Related Careers: Chemist, Physicist, Planetary Scientist

Atmospheric scientists study weather and climate. These scientists predict weather, work in the field to collect climate and weather data, or develop equipment. Atmospheric chemists study the atoms and molecules in the atmosphere. Climatologists study long-term climate and the climate in Earth's past. Atmospheric science is used to study the atmospheres and weather on other planets and moons. Satellites are also very important for studying and predicting Earth's climate and weather. Atmospheric science combines parts of chemistry, biology, modelling, and physics.

Atmospheric scientists use satellites to study hurricanes like this one.

Career Pioneer: Eunice Foote

Eunice Foote (1819-1888) was an atmospheric scientist who contributed to the discovery of the greenhouse effect. Foote was an amateur scientist and did not have any college education. In 1856, she performed an experiment showing that moist air warmed faster than dry air. Carbon dioxide warmed faster than both. This concept is the foundation of the greenhouse effect, a very important climatic process.[7]

Left: A drawing of Eunice Foote. There are no known photographs of her.

Atmospheric Scientist

Professional Profile: Dr. Yolanda Shea

NAME: Yolanda Shea

CAREER: Atmospheric Scientist

EDUCATION:

- Bachelor's: Earth and Atmospheric Science, Cornell University
- Master's: Atmospheric and Oceanic Science, University of Colorado
- Ph.D.: Atmospheric and Oceanic Science, University of Colorado

EMPLOYER: NASA

TITLE: Atmospheric Research Scientist

"We can think of our eyes as remote sensing 'instruments' that are sensitive to reflected light."

Dr. Yolanda Shea specializes in using remote sensing to study Earth. In particular, she is interested in how reflected sunlight can be used to analyze Earth's climate. Dr. Shea currently works with the CPF mission, which will take very accurate measurements of reflected sunlight from the International Space Station. Previously, Shea worked with the Climate Absolute Radiance and Refractivity Observatory (CLARREO) mission. She has enjoyed "growing up" with CPF from graduate school to now leading a NASA team.

Dr. Shea has been honored with numerous awards including the Presidential Early Career Award for Scientists and Engineers. She also was awarded the Women of Color in STEM Technology Rising Star Award. In her free time, Dr. Shea enjoys practicing the violin, which she has played since middle school.

Chemical Engineer

Related Careers: Aerospace Engineer, Chemist, Materials Engineer

Chemical engineers produce chemicals, medicines, fuel, foods, and materials. Chemical engineers may work to process raw materials into finished products or to create new chemicals in the laboratory. These engineers also protect the environment and manage hazardous materials. Chemical engineers are important to the space industry. They help make rocket fuel, paints to protect spacecraft, and more. Most chemical engineers work in private industry, but some may work in government research. Chemical engineers use computer modelling, chemistry, math, and physics.

Chemical engineers work with rockets like the Space Shuttle to develop fuels and protect the vehicle from heat and harsh chemicals.

Career Pioneer: Elisa Leonida Zamfirescu

Elisa Leonida Zamfirescu (1887-1973) was one of the first women to earn an engineering degree. She attended the Royal Academy of Technology Berlin despite considerable opposition. Zamfirescu joined the Geological Institute of Romania, eventually leading 12 laboratories. She pioneered new techniques for analyzing minerals and discovered new natural resources. She was the first female member of the General Association of Romanian Engineers.[8]

Left: Elisa Leonida Zamfirescu

Chemical Engineer

Professional Profile: Kate Doetsch

NAME: Kate Doetsch

CAREER: Chemical Engineer

EDUCATION:
- Bachelor's: Chemical Engineering, University of Missouri

EMPLOYER: The Boeing Company

TITLE: Materials & Process Engineer

> "Engineering is such a fulfilling career with so many potential pathways."

Kate Doetsch is a chemical engineer specializing in sealants and finishes to prevent corrosion on commercial and defense aircraft. She previously worked to analyze the environmental effects on the materials of the Space Launch System rocket.

Ms. Doetsch has been honored with several awards. She was a guest lecturer at and received an award from the University of Missouri. She was also named a New Emerging Leader in Technology and Engineering (ELiTE) by the Society of Women Engineers. She previously led the Society of Women Engineers (SWE) Outreach Committee. Ms. Doetsch was inspired to pursue engineering by her father, who is also an engineer. She chose chemical engineering because of her love of math, physics, and chemistry, particularly electrochemistry. She enjoys cooking, baking, working out, and in fall 2020 welcomed her first child.

Chemist

Related Careers: Astrobiologist, Chemical Engineer, Planetary Scientist

Chemists study the structure and properties of substances. They use that information to create new products. Chemistry research has improved everything from medicines to plastics and batteries. Some chemists, like analytical and forensic chemists, use chemistry to identify unknown substances. Others study known chemicals to learn about their properties. Chemistry is used in the space industry for developing new materials, studying samples from other planets, improving rocket fuel, and other applications. Chemists use math, computer modelling, chemistry, and physics.

Spacecraft like *Cassini* are used to learn about the chemistry of planets and moons.

Career Pioneer: Marie Curie

Marie Curie (1867-1934) was a chemist and physicist known for her work in the field of radioactivity. In 1903, she received the Nobel Prize in Physics with two other scientists. This was awarded for their discovery of radioactivity. Alone, she also earned the 1911 Nobel Prize in Chemistry for isolating pure radium. Later in her career, she turned to the use of radioactivity in medicine. She was the first woman to win a Nobel Prize and remains the only woman to win the award in two different fields.

[9] **Left: Marie Curie circa 1920.**

Chemist

Professional Profile: Dr. Morgan Cable

NAME: Morgan Cable

CAREER: Chemist

EDUCATION:

- Bachelor's: Chemistry, Florida Atlantic University

- Ph.D.: Inorganic Chemistry, California Institute of Technology

EMPLOYER: NASA's Jet Propulsion Laboratory

TITLE: Ocean Worlds Program Scientist

"I'M ALWAYS LEARNING AS WE DEVELOP MISSIONS TO EXPLORE NEW PLACES IN THE SOLAR SYSTEM AND BEYOND."

Dr. Morgan Cable is a chemist specializing in planetary science. Dr. Cable works with the MISE instrument on the Europa Clipper Mission. She is also a member of the science team for the Dragonfly Mission to Saturn's moon Titan. Dr. Cable previously worked on the Cassini mission to Saturn. At the end of that mission, Cassini underwent a planned crash into Saturn to intentionally destroy the spacecraft. Dr. Cable and her colleagues "watched as Cassini hurtled into Saturn's atmosphere" in the early morning. Dr. Cable was invited to be a commentator on NASA TV as the finale was broadcasted.

She was named one of the "Talented Twelve" rising stars in Chemistry by the American Chemical Society. She is also a Fellow of a program called "Signatures of Life in the Universe." She was inspired by her father, also a NASA chemist, and other mentors. She enjoys surfing, mountain unicycling, and piloting Cessna 172s.

Computer Scientist

Related Careers: Electrical Engineer, Mission Controller, Robotics Engineer

Computer scientists work on many different projects on Earth and in space. Some design, develop, and improve computers, software, and more. Computer programmers and software developers write and test computer code. This code provides instructions to everything from cell phones to Mars rovers. Computer scientists are extremely important in space exploration. Computer scientists program satellites and probes, design navigation, and ensure that mission control has data about spacecraft. Computer scientists use math, computer programming, and logic skills.

Computer scientists work with spacecraft like the *Europa Clipper Mission*.

Career Pioneer: Grace Hopper

Grace Hopper (1906-1992) helped create the first commercial electronic computer. She studied at Vassar College and earned a Ph.D. from Yale before joining the Naval Reserve. There, she worked on the Mark I, an early calculator and computer. She also designed a software that converted programming into code that could be used by a computer. She was awarded the National Medal of Technology and the Presidential Medal of Freedom for her work.[10]

Left: Hopper in 1984

COMPUTER SCIENTIST

PROFESSIONAL PROFILE: MELISSA SORIANO

NAME: Melissa Soriano

CAREER: Computer Scientist

EDUCATION:
- Bachelor's: Electrical and Computer Engineering, California Institute of Technology
- Master's: Earth Science, George Mason University

EMPLOYER: NASA's Jet Propulsion Laboratory

TITLE: Payload System Engineer

> "KEEP FOLLOWING YOUR PASSION AND DREAMS. WORK HARD AND STAY FOCUSED, AND YOU WILL HAVE LIMITLESS OPPORTUNITIES."

Melissa Soriano is a computer and electrical engineer who specializes in deep space communications. She previously served as a software engineer. Ms. Soriano worked with the Mars Science Laboratory (Curiosity rover) and the Mars 2020 mission (Perseverance rover). She developed programs for communications with Earth during entry, descent, and landing. She works on the telecommunications system of the Europa Clipper Mission. She enjoys the challenges and the unique work of her field.

Ms. Soriano was inspired to pursue her current career by her mother. She enjoys spending time outdoors, both hiking and relaxing at the beach.

> "MY FAVORITE ASPECTS OF THIS FIELD ARE THE PEOPLE WHO ARE SO PASSIONATE ABOUT WHAT WE DO, THE CHALLENGES, AND THE UNIQUE WORK."

Electrical Engineer

Related Careers: Aerospace Engineer, Computer Scientist, Mechanical Engineer

Electrical engineers work with electrical equipment, electrical systems, and computers. These professionals design and test electronic components like motors, batteries, and circuits. Electrical engineers also work with equipment like radar and GPS. Electrical engineers are very important in the space industry. They design fuel cells, solar panels, computerized navigation for rockets, and specialized sensors. Most electrical engineers work in private industry, but some work for the government or military. Electrical engineers study and use computer modelling, mathematics, and physics.

Electrical engineers help design and build all types of rockets, like this Atlas V.

Career Pioneer: Hedy Lamarr

Hedy Lamarr (1914-2000) was an Austrian-born actress and the inventor of a technology that is the foundation of Wi-Fi today. Before moving to America, Lamarr and her then-husband attended meetings about military inventions. This was the beginning of Lamarr's interest in technology. During World War II, Lamarr learned of the US Navy's challenges with torpedoes. Lamarr's invention, called the Secret Communication System, was adopted in the 1960s.[11]

Left: Lamarr in a 1944 film.

Electrical Engineer

Professional Profile: Rachel Morford

NAME: Rachel Morford

CAREER: Electrical Engineer

EDUCATION:

- Bachelor's: Electrical Engineering, University of Southern California

- Master's: Electrical Engineering, University of Southern California

EMPLOYER: The Aerospace Corporation

TITLE: Principal Director of Missile Warning Capability Integration

"I love working on very complex and challenging problems with incredibly smart people!"

Rachel Morford is a space systems engineer with a background in electrical engineering. While working on her master's, she worked at NASA's Jet Propulsion Lab. There, she analyzed data from the TERRA satellite. At the Aerospace Corporation, she has worked with Atlas V and Delta IV rockets. She also coordinated with the Air Force to develop international agreements to share data.

Ms. Morford was a part of mission control for three satellite launches. She monitored the spacecraft before, during, and after launch. Since she was "on-console," she got to call out that she was "Go" for launch! Ms. Morford has earned awards through the Society of Women Engineers and elsewhere. She was inspired to study engineering by stargazing and a high school electronics class. She enjoys doing outreach events with the Society of Women Engineers.

Geologist

Related Careers: Astrobiologist, Chemist, Planetary Scientist

Geologists, or geoscientists, study the composition and structure of the Earth and the processes that have shaped it. Some geologists do fieldwork, meaning they travel to, collect samples from, and study specific locations. Some geologists study rocks and minerals, volcanoes, earthquakes, or ancient fossils. Geology is important to planetary science so scientists can study the formation and evolution of other planetary bodies. Additionally, some geoscientists use satellites to map and study the Earth from above. Geologists use aspects of chemistry, biology, physics, and math.

Geologists think hydrothermal vents like this may host life deep in the ocean of the moon Europa.

Career Pioneer: Marie Tharp

Marie Tharp (1920-2006) was an American geologist who helped to create the first map of the ocean floor. In 1946, she earned her master's degree in Geology. After graduating, she joined the Lamont Geological Laboratory at Columbia University. There, Tharp would painstakingly draw intricate maps of the seafloor based on her colleagues' data. This demonstrated that the ocean floor is not flat. This was critical proof of the theory of plate tectonics.[12]

Left: Marie Tharp

Geologist

Professional Profile: Dr. Lauren Edgar

NAME: Lauren Edgar

CAREER: Geologist

EDUCATION:
- Bachelor's: Earth Sciences, Dartmouth College
- Master's: Geology, California Institute of Technology
- Ph.D.: Geology, California Institute of Technology

EMPLOYER: United States Geological Survey

TITLE: Research Geologist

"Every day there's the potential to see something new that no one has ever seen before on Mars."

Dr. Lauren Edgar specializes in sedimentology and stratigraphy. This means she analyzes materials like clay and sand as well as layers of rock. Dr. Edgar worked with NASA's Mars Exploration Rover mission. During that mission, the rover started to drag its wheel through Mars's dirt. Fortunately, this problem allowed the team to discover new minerals on Mars! Dr. Edgar is currently a member of the Mars Science Laboratory mission where she works to analyze data from the Curiosity rover. She advocates for science activities and trains NASA personnel in geology.

Dr. Edgar has received awards from NASA and USGS. She was inspired by watching a Space Shuttle launch and meeting an Apollo astronaut, and she decided to pursue geology after a research project about meteorites. Dr. Edgar has done fieldwork everywhere from Antarctica to Oman and the Alps. In her free time, she enjoys hiking, running, kayaking, yoga, and cooking.

Materials Engineer

Related Careers: Aerospace Engineer, Chemical Engineer, Chemist

Materials engineers develop, test, and study materials. These materials are used for sports equipment, computers, airplanes, and other purposes. Materials engineers also help select what products to use for different applications based on the needs of the project and properties of the material. Many specialized materials are important for building and protecting rockets, satellites, or spacesuits. Most materials engineers work in private industry, but some work for universities and the government. Materials engineers often use chemistry, math, and physics.

Tiles made of a special ceramic material were used to protect the space shuttle.

Career Pioneer: Stephanie Kwolek

Stephanie Kwolek (1923-2014) was an American chemist and the inventor of Kevlar. After graduating college, Kwolek applied to work at chemical manufacturer DuPont. While working at DuPont, Kwolek discovered liquid crystalline solutions. One of these was spun into an incredibly strong fiber now known as Kevlar. Kevlar is now used in body armor, communications equipment, sports gear, and more.[13]

Left: Stephanie Kwolek at Spinning Elements by Harry Kalish, licensed under CC BY-SA 3.0

Materials Engineer

Professional Profile: Dr. Mary Kinsella

NAME: Mary Kinsella

CAREER: Materials Engineer

EDUCATION:
- Bachelor's: Manufacturing Technology, Miami University
- Master's: Materials Engineering, University of Dayton
- Ph.D.: Industrial and Systems Engineering, Ohio State University

EMPLOYER: Air Force Research Laboratory (former)

TITLE: Senior Manufacturing Research Engineer

> "I liked having an impact and making a difference in leading-edge technologies."

Dr. Mary Kinsella worked as an engineer and team leader researching aerospace materials. She also was a part of other aspects of aerospace research and development. Earlier in her career, she worked in the microelectronics industry. She also explored 3D printing for space applications. Today, Dr. Kinsella owns her own company coaching women in engineering and science. She recently edited a book about women's work in aerospace materials.

Working in the aerospace field, Dr. Kinsella had the chance to tour the space shuttle payload facility. She also got to watch a shuttle launch! Currently, she is a Fellow of the Society of Women Engineers. She is also a pianist and violinist and enjoys knitting, sewing, puzzling, and do-it-yourself projects.

> "If you're interested in the space field, follow your dream!"

Mechanical Engineer

Related Careers: Aerospace Engineer, Electrical Engineer, Robotics Engineer

Mechanical engineering is one of the broadest fields in the world of engineering. Mechanical engineers design, build, and test machines. These engineers work with cars, airplanes, generators, batteries, and much more. Mechanical engineers work in energy, safety, transportation, and beyond! Many mechanical engineers work in manufacturing or as consultants. In the space industry, mechanical engineers design aspects of rockets, satellites, launch pads, and other important equipment. These engineers often use physics, math, chemistry, and even computer modelling.

Mechanical engineers help design aircraft and spacecraft like the HTV-2.

Career Pioneer: Beulah Henry

Beulah Henry (1887-1973) invented numerous devices to make everyday life easier. Henry did not have any formal education, yet she was granted a total of 49 patents. Her inventions include an ice cream freezer, a document copying device, and an improved sewing machine. She also created a clock to teach children to tell time and a doll whose eyes changed color. Known as the "Lady Edison," Henry was inducted into the National Inventors Hall of Fame.[14]

Left: Beulah Henry with one of her inventions.

28

MECHANICAL ENGINEER

PROFESSIONAL PROFILE: MARY BETH BIDDLE

NAME: Mary Beth Biddle

CAREER: Mechanical Engineer

EDUCATION:
- Bachelor's: Mechanical Engineering, University of Pittsburg
- Master's: Mechanical Engineering, Villanova University

EMPLOYER: Lockheed Martin

TITLE: Project Engineer

> "YOU CAN DO IT! SPACE IS AN EXCITING AREA, AND YOU'LL BRING VALUABLE KNOWLEDGE AND A DIVERSE WAY OF THINKING TO THE FIELD!"

Mary Beth Biddle started at Lockheed Martin as a mechanical engineer, and now leads projects. Her specialty is structural analysis. She evaluates the temperatures and pressures a space vehicle experiences during flight. She then determines if the aircraft will survive the flight, and, if not, makes recommendations to redesign it. She worked on the Falcon HTV-2 vehicle, which flies at Mach 20 (13,000 miles per hour). At that speed, the HTV-2 could travel between New York and Los Angeles in 12 minutes!

Ms. Biddle has serval earned awards for her work and was named an Emerging Leader in Technology and Engineering by the Society of Women Engineers. Ms. Biddle was inspired to study engineering by a program led by women engineers while she was in elementary school. She loves to travel and has visited all 50 states. While travelling, she learns about other cultures, tries new foods, and enjoys hiking.

Mission Controller

Related Careers: Aerospace Engineer, Computer Scientist, Planetary Scientist

Mission controllers and mission operations experts are critical to space exploration. Mission controllers plan, organize, and practice launches and operations. Mission control has many experts who specialize in areas like navigation, electronics, and fuel. Mission operations is also essential for robotic missions without astronauts. Mission operations specialists often write complicated computer programs to plan a rover's or satellite's exploration tasks. People who work in mission control and operations must have strong teamwork and relevant technical skills.

Mission operations specialists program and control spacecraft like the *Parker Solar Probe*.

Career Pioneer: Frances "Poppy" Northcutt

Frances "Poppy" Northcutt (1943-) was the first woman to work in NASA mission control. After graduating from the University of Texas, Northcutt became a "computress" with NASA. She performed calculations for the Gemini program. For the Apollo program, she and her team planned the trajectory to return the astronauts to Earth. She was the only woman working in mission control for Apollo 8. Later in her career, Northcutt became a women's rights activist and attorney.[15]

Left: Northcutt in Mission Control

Mission Controller

Professional Profile: Sarah Hamilton

NAME: Sarah Hamilton

CAREER: Mission Operations Specialist

EDUCATION:
- Bachelor's: Aerospace Engineering, Syracuse University
- Master's: Software Engineering, University of Maryland University College

EMPLOYER: Johns Hopkins University Applied Physics Laboratory

TITLE: Mission Operations Analyst

"I remember seeing the first image of Pluto that we downlinked at closest approach on July 14th, and it was an amazing moment. It felt like a dream and I had to pinch myself to believe I helped with that."

Sarah Hamilton works in the field of mission operations for deep space spacecraft. She works with NASA's New Horizons and Parker Solar Probe missions. Ms. Hamilton served as a flight controller for the TERRA EOS AM-1 Spacecraft. As flight controller, she monitored spacecraft data with a team of colleagues. She also worked to program the NASA MESSENGER probe that visited Mercury. In her words, "these spacecraft become your children."

For her work, Ms. Hamilton received awards from NASA and International SpaceOps. She was inspired by watching Halley's Comet and meteor showers. Loving aviation, she flew remote-control airplanes and earned her pilot's license. She also enjoys photography and outdoor adventures like hiking and skiing.

Physicist

Related Careers: Astronomer & Astrophysicist, Chemist, Mechanical Engineer

Physicists study matter, energy, light, electricity, and more. Theoretical physicists develop theories and models to explain the universe. Experimental physicists plan and execute experiments . Then, these scientists present their findings in scholarly journals, conferences, and lectures. Many physicists work with astronomers and astrophysicists to uncover the laws of physics across the galaxy and universe. Physics is important for planning missions, designing rockets, and understanding astronomy. Physicists work with computer modelling and math, and they must study physics.

Physicists use tools like LIGO to test theories of the universe.

Career Pioneer: Chien-Shiung Wu

Chien-Shiung Wu (1912-1997) was a Chinese-American nuclear physicist. She began her education in China before moving to the United States. She earned her Ph.D. from the University of California, Berkeley. Relocating to the east coast, Wu became a physics professor at Princeton University. Wu then joined the Manhattan Project performing critical physics research. Her later experiments proved important nuclear physics theories. There is an asteroid named after her.[16]

Left: Wu in 1958.

PHYSICIST

PROFESSIONAL PROFILE: DR. LAURA CADONATI

NAME: Laura Cadonati

CAREER: Physicist

EDUCATION:
- Bachelor's: Physics, Universita' degli Studi (Milan, Italy)
- Master's: Physics, Princeton University
- Ph.D.: Physics, Princeton University

EMPLOYER: Georgia Institute of Technology

TITLE: Professor of Physics

"I WAS INTRIGUED BY THE POSSIBILITY TO EXPLAIN REALITY AROUND ME AND MAKE PREDICTIONS."

Dr. Laura Cadonati is a physicist specializing in data analysis. She is also the Director for the Center of Relativistic Astrophysics at Georgia Tech. She works on data analysis for the LIGO project, which discovered gravitational waves. The project's founders were awarded the Nobel Prize. With that team, Dr. Cadonati earned numerous awards such as the Physics World Breakthrough of the Year and the Breakthrough Prize in Fundamental Physics, among others.

Dr. Cadonati was inspired to pursue physics by other female scientists from Italy. She enjoys patchwork quilting and baking and spends much of her spare time with her children.

"BELIEVE IN YOURSELF AND FIND YOUR SUPPORT NETWORK; FIND MENTORS AND PEERS THAT YOU CAN ASK QUESTIONS OR TEST YOUR IDEAS WITH."

Pilot

Related Careers: Aerospace Engineer, Astronaut, Mission Controller

Pilots are important in space exploration because many astronauts start their careers as airplane or helicopter pilots. Some astronauts are responsible for flying and maneuvering the spacecraft. Astronauts with this role begin by piloting airplanes or helicopters and must have 1,000 hours of flight time to qualify. The first Americans to fly into space were all military test pilots. Pilots can also work for commercial airlines. Pilots also fly private airplanes, lead charter flights, or do agricultural work like crop dusting. Some people also fly airplanes, helicopters, or gliders as a hobby.

Astronaut Curtis Brown practices piloting the Space Shuttle.

Career Pioneer: Jerrie Cobb

Jerrie Cobb (1931-2019) was a member of the Mercury 13, a group of 13 women who trained as NASA astronauts. Cobb had an early interest in airplanes and earned her pilot's license at age 16. She struggled to find a piloting job that would allow women. As an aerobatic pilot, she set several aviation records. At age 28, Cobb joined the Mercury 13 where she underwent the Mercury astronaut training process. She successfully completed every task, yet she was never allowed to be an astronaut.[17] Left: Cobb poses next to a Mercury spacecraft.

PILOT

CAREER PIONEER: EILEEN COLLINS

Eileen Collins (1956-) is a former NASA astronaut and was the first woman to pilot and command a space shuttle. Collins had an early love of aviation, and she earned a degree in mathematics. She became an Air Force pilot and flight instructor and was later selected and trained as an astronaut. In 1995, she piloted the space shuttle Discovery and in 1999, she commanded the space shuttle Columbia.

Left: Collins in 1998.

STORY SPOTLIGHT: JASMIN MOGHBELI

As part of her training, astronaut and former Marine Corps pilot Jasmin Moghbeli trained in NASA's Neutral Buoyancy Laboratory. In her words:

"For me, the first time getting in a spacesuit and training for a spacewalk in the Neutral Buoyancy Lab (i.e., really large pool with a life-sized mockup of the International Space Station) was really eye-opening. I had previously watched videos of astronauts performing real spacewalks and they had made it look relatively easy. But it was unlike anything I had ever done before and, initially, I found it exhausting. Learning how to work with the suit, rather than fighting against it, was one of the most challenging aspects of astronaut training for me. Yet, at the same time, getting to fulfill my lifelong dream of becoming an astronaut and put on a spacesuit was surreal. It is a perfect example of how this job can be very challenging, but also extremely rewarding." **Above: Moghbeli training at the Neutral Buoyancy Laboratory**

Planetary Scientist

Related Careers: Astrobiologist, Atmospheric Scientist, Geologist

Planetary science is the study of planets and planetary systems. Planetary scientists study moons, planets' rings, atmospheres, magnetic fields, and more. They can specialize in astrobiology, atmospheric science, or geology. Planetary scientists work to answer questions about how the solar system, planets, and their moons formed and evolved. They do this with telescopes, satellites, and rovers. Planetary scientists also build computer models and perform experiments in labs on Earth. The field combines aspects of chemistry, geology, physics, biology, and astronomy.

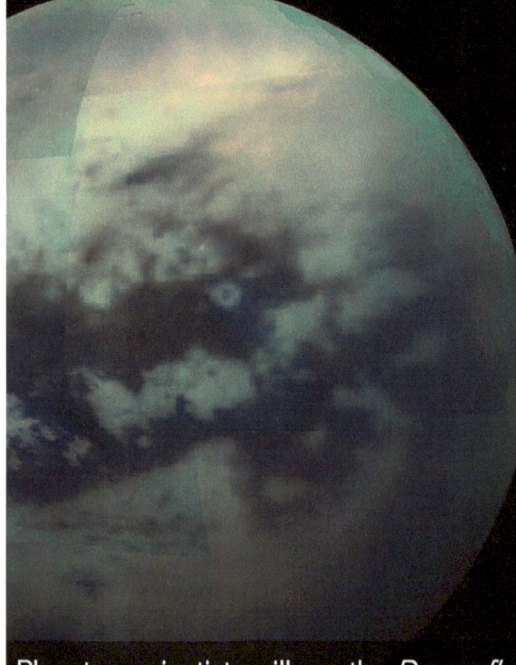

Planetary scientists will use the *Dragonfly* mission to study Saturn's moon Titan.

Career Pioneer: Caroline Herschel

Caroline Herschel (1750-1848) was a German astronomer and planetary scientist. Herschel assisted her brother William with his work in astronomy. The siblings worked together to build their own telescopes. Caroline also performed complex calculations for her brother and her own observations. Together, the siblings discovered the planet Uranus in 1781. Caroline Herschel was also the first woman to discover a comet and the first professional woman astronomer.[18]

Left: Herschel in 1829

Planetary Scientist

Professional Profile: Dr. Jennifer Stern

NAME: Jennifer Stern

CAREER: Planetary Scientist

EDUCATION:

- Bachelor's: Geology-Biology, Brown University

- Ph.D.: Geochemistry, Florida State University

EMPLOYER: NASA Goddard Space Flight Center

TITLE: Space Research Scientist

"Planetary science is all about exploration and probing the unknown."

Dr. Jennifer Stern is a planetary scientist with NASA's Goddard Space Flight Center in Maryland. Dr. Stern is a stable isotope geochemist who looks for evidence of life or of chemical processes on Mars. Currently, she is a member of the Curiosity rover team and focuses on the Sample Analysis at Mars, or SAM, instrument. For 90 days after Curiosity landed, Dr. Stern and her colleagues at NASA had to live and work on Mars time. Mars days are 40 minutes longer than days on Earth! She also recently began working on NASA's Dragonfly mission, which will study Saturn's moon Titan.

In 2015, Dr. Stern was honored with the Presidential Early Career Award for Scientists and Engineers. She was inspired to study geology after her childhood skiing in the mountains of Colorado and Utah. Dr. Stern also enjoys hobbies from Middle Eastern dance to improv and printmaking.

ROBOTICS ENGINEER

Related Careers: Aerospace Engineer, Computer Scientist, Mechanical Engineer

Robotics engineers are a type of engineer, many of whom also use computer programming skills. They specialize in designing, building, maintaining, and using robots. Robotics engineers plan how robots move, obtain information, and perform tasks. Robots are very important in space exploration. Robotics engineers work with the Mars rovers, the International Space Station, and more. Robotics engineers also work in other fields, such as automobile manufacturing and other assembly lines. Robotics engineers use aspects of materials science, physics, and computer programming.

Robotics engineers design and program rovers like NASA's *Spirit* and *Opportunity*.

CAREER PIONEER: ADA LOVELACE

Ada Lovelace (1815-1852) is known as the first computer programmer. She was educated by tutors and studied with a professor of mathematics. Lovelace was interested in the early computers of Charles Babbage. Her notes described how the machine could be programmed to perform math calculations. This rudimentary work is the foundation of all computer programming, and by extension, all robotics.[19]

Left: Lovelace circa 1840

Robotics Engineer

Professional Profile: Julie Townsend

NAME: Julie Townsend

CAREER: Robotics Engineer

EDUCATION:

- Bachelor's: Aeronautics and Astronautics, Massachusetts Institute of Technology
- Master's: Aeronautics and Astronautics, Stanford University

EMPLOYER: NASA's Jet Propulsion Laboratory

TITLE: Robotics System Engineer

"I enjoy the challenges of creating robots that stretch the limits of what is possible."

Julie Townsend is a robotics system engineer specializing in aerospace robotics. She leads the group of engineers which controls the Perseverance Rover collecting samples from Mars. Ms. Townsend started at NASA's Jet Propulsion Laboratory (JPL) working with the electronics and sensors of the Spirit and Opportunity rovers. She planned the daily activities of the rovers. During Mars's spring, the team on Earth saw the Spirit rover's power decrease. Sadly, they thought the rover "was declining to an inevitable end." One morning, Ms. Townsend was surprised to see that Spirit's power had been restored! Winds on Mars had cleaned the rover's solar panels. Ms. Townsend has also contributed to experimental robotics projects. Ms. Townsend was inspired as a teen by a program at Purdue University. In her free time, Ms. Townsend coaches robotics teams with Girl Scouts. This allows girls to explore engineering, programming, and robotics.

Space Medicine Specialist

Related Careers: Astrobiologist, Chemist, Mechanical Engineer

Space medicine is a broad field that focuses on keeping astronauts healthy. Scientists in this field may specialize in biology, nutrition, exercise, medicine, and more. Many space medicine specialists are physicians. Physicians, also known as medical doctors, identify and treat sicknesses and injuries. They study medical histories, prescribe medicines, examine patients, and perform procedures like surgery. Doctors can work in many specialized areas. Experts in the space medicine field study biology, and some also use chemistry, computer modelling, and medical skills.

Astronaut Sunni Williams exercises using a specially-designed treadmill on the International Space Station.

Career Pioneer: Mae Jemison

Mae Jemison (1956-) was a physician and the first African-American female astronaut. She earned her bachelor's degree from Stanford University and her medical degree from Cornell University. After graduating, she worked as a medical officer with the Peace Corps. In 1986, she was selected to be an astronaut. She spent a week in space aboard the space shuttle Endeavour. She served as an astronaut for six years and currently works with several nonprofits.[20]

Left: Jemison in 1992

SPACE MEDICINE SPECIALIST

PROFESSIONAL PROFILE: DR. DORIT DONOVIEL

NAME: Dorit Donoviel

CAREER: Space Medicine Specialist

EDUCATION:
- Bachelor's: Biochemistry and Cell Biology, University of California
- Ph.D.: Biochemistry, University of Washington

EMPLOYER: Baylor College of Medicine

TITLE: Associate Professor

"The challenges of spaceflight really force us to innovate around health and human performance for Earth as well."

Dr. Dorit Donoviel works in the field of space medicine. She is the Director of the Translation Research Institute for Space Health. She is a native of Israel but now lives in Houston, Texas. Dr. Donoviel led a $250 million research project for NASA. The program focused on biomedical research that would allow humans to safely explore deep space.

Dr. Donoviel was honored with the NASA Human Research Program Peer Award. Additionally, she received the Pioneer Award from the National Space Biomedical Research Institute. Dr. Donoviel was inspired by her high school biology teacher. Since she loves exploring all aspects of biology, she SCUBA dives in her free time.

"Don't be afraid to ask people to help you."

OTHER CAREERS TO CONSIDER

Aerospace is a broad industry that includes many more careers than those detailed here. For those who are interested in space, there are countless other career paths to consider. People with a wide variety of specialties and interests are crucial to space exploration. Other space-related careers include:

Artists & Photographers: Pictures and diagrams are essential for communicating with the public. Artists design logos and create images of everything from rockets to exoplanets, and photographers document launches and other milestones.

Artists create images like this to share discoveries of exoplanets with the public.

International Relations Experts: Space exploration is multinational. Specialists are needed to negotiate and communicate with the governments and space programs of other countries.

Nutritionists & Chefs: Nutritionists and chefs are needed to plan and prepare meals for astronauts. These specialists ensure that astronauts consume all the nutrients they need.

Public Policy Specialists: NASA receives its funding from the U.S. Congress, so talented people must advocate for NASA to ensure it receives the money it needs to continue its missions.

Technicians: In every engineering field, technicians are needed to build models for testing and full-size rockets and spacecraft like rovers and satellites. Engineers may design these, but someone has to build them.

Writers: Technical writers are necessary to clearly explain ideas and missions to the public, investors, and other stakeholders through countless press releases, web pages, and technical reports.

Advice & Inspiration

On Passion:

If you are doing something you truly enjoy, you'll make it! (Heather Wiest)

The most important thing to have is curiosity and passion. Just keep asking questions about what interests you. (Dr. Jennifer Stern)

Find something you love to do! (Dr. Morgan Cable)

Work hard, stay curious, pursue your interests, and you'll have fun along your journey. (Dr. Yolanda Shea)

On Perseverance:

It's not always going to be easy. But stay true to yourself and who you are, put in the hard work, and you can do anything you put your mind to! (Kerstin Diesch)

Learn firsthand that theory isn't perfect, the first attempt is almost always flawed, every failure brings a gift of understanding, and perseverance will eventually achieve the goal. (Julie Townsend)

When something feels hard, it doesn't mean you are not smart. It's a challenge to learn from and overcome. (Sarah Hamilton)

It is important to recognize that you will likely have setbacks or failures along the way that may make you doubt yourself. Know that this is very common and just means you are pushing yourself to your limits, which will only make you grow. (Major Jasmin Moghbeli)

Keep in mind that career paths aren't always clear, straight paths. There are often twists and turns along the way, and it's okay if your interests change as you progress, too! (Dr. Yolanda Shea)

Advice & Inspiration

On Support & Teamwork:

Find others who are also interested in STEM and support each other in your interests! (Rachel Morford)

Stick with the people who support you. Don't let anyone discourage you from pursuing what you are interested in. (Dr. Jennifer Stern)

Surround yourself with supportive people and peers and don't be shy to ask questions. (Kristina McCarthy)

Reach out to everyone that you find interesting and ask for advice or for connections. (Dr. Dorit Donoviel)

Let people know what you're interested in and ask for their help! It can be so helpful to have someone who advocates for you, and who can mentor you along the way. But you may have to go out and find that advocate or ask someone to be your mentor. (Katelyn Boushon)

Regardless of the field you're interested in, always have someone to support you. You don't have to go through this journey alone. (Dr. Yolanda Shea)

On Believing in Yourself:

If you're interested in the space field, follow your dream! Set a goal and achieve it! Girls your age have great ideas and many skills.
(Dr. Mary Kinsella)

Don't let other people set your limits.
(Katelyn Boushon)

Never give up on yourself and your dreams! (Major Jasmin Moghbeli)

Do not be afraid to try, have faith, believe in yourself, and do not be afraid to ask for help. (Sarah Hamilton)

Name Index

Biddle, Mary Beth, 30
Boushon, Katelyn, 45
Brodsky, Julia, 10
Cable, Morgan, 20, 44
Cadonati, Laura, 34
Cobb, Jerrie, 35
Collins, Eileen, 36
Curie, Marie, 19
Diesch, Kerstin, 44
Doetsch, Kate, 18
Donoviel, Dorit, 42, 45
Edgar, Lauren, 26
Foote, Eunice, 15
Franklin, Rosalind, 9
Hamilton, Sarah, 32, 44, 45
Henry, Beulah, 29
Herschel, Caroline, 37
Hopper, Grace, 21
Jackson, Mary, 7
Jemison, Mae, 41
Kinsella, Mary, 28, 45
Kwolek, Stephanie, 27
Lamarr, Hedy, 23
Lovelace, Ada, 39
McCarthy, Kristina, 45
Moghbeli, Jasmin, 12, 36, 44, 45
Morford, Rachel, 24, 45
Northcutt, Frances "Poppy", 31
Rubin, Vera, 13
Shea, Yolanda, 16, 44, 45
Soriano, Melissa, 22
Stern, Jennifer, 38, 44, 45
Tereshkova, Valentina, 11
Tharp, Marie, 25
Townsend, Julie, 40, 44
Vieregg, Abigail, 14
Wiest, Heather, 8, 44
Wu, Chien-Shiung, 33
Zamfirescu, Elisa Leonida, 17

References

The Bureau of Labor Statistics is a fascinating and thorough resource for data about thousands of careers. All data about typical jobs, responsibilities, work environments, and education comes from the BLS, accessible at bls.org.

[1] Chambers, D. W. (1983). Stereotypic images of the scientist. The Draw-a-Scientist Test. *Science Education Assessment Instruments.* onlinelibrary.wiley.com/doi/epdf/10.1002/sce.3730670213.

[2] Hollingham, R. (2019). Apollo in 50 numbers: The workers. *BBC.* bbc.com/future/article/20190617-apollo-in-50-numbers-the-workers.

[3] Tikkanen, A. (2021). Mary Jackson. *Encyclopedia Britannica.* britannica.com/biography/Mary-Jackson-mathematician-and-engineer.

References (Continued)

[4]The Editors of Encyclopedia Britannica. (2021). Rosalind Franklin. *Encyclopedia Britannica*. britannica.com/biography/Rosalind-Franklin.

[5]National Air and Space Museum. (n.d.). Valentina Tereshkova. *National Air and Space Museum*. airandspace.si.edu/people/historical-figure/valentina-tereshkova.

[6]Childers, T. (2019). Vera Rubin: The astronomer who brought dark matter to light. *Space.com*. space.com/vera-rubin.html.

[7]Schwartz, J. (2020). Overlooked no more: Eunice Foote, climate scientist lost to history. *The New York Times*. nytimes.com/2020/04/21/obituaries/eunice-foote-overlooked.html.

[8]Europeana. (n.d.). Elisa Leonida Zamfirescu. *Europeana*. europeana.eu/hr/exhibitions/pioneers/elisa-leonida-zamfirescu.

[9]The Editors of Encyclopedia Britannica. (2021). Marie Curie. *Encyclopedia Britannica*. britannica.com/biography/Marie-Curie.

[10]The Editors of Encyclopedia Britannica. (2021). Grace Hopper. *Encyclopedia Britannica*. britannica.com/biography/Grace-Hopper.

[11]Kratz, J. (2020). The world war II-era actress who invented wi-fi: Hedy Lamarr. *National Archives*. prologue.blogs.archives.gov/2020/05/26/the-world-war-ii-era-actress-that-invented-wi-fi-hedy-lamarr/.

[12]The Mariner's Museum and Park. (n.d.). Marie Tharp. *The Mariner's Museum and Park*. exploration.marinersmuseum.org/subject/marie-tharp/.

[13]Science History Institute. (2017). Stephanie L. Kwolek. *Science History Institute*. sciencehistory.org/historical-profile/stephanie-l-kwolek.

[14]National Inventors Hall of Fame. (n.d.). Beulah Louise Henry. *National Inventors Hall of Fame*. https://www.invent.org/inductees/beulah-louise-henry.

[15]Waxman, O. (2019). Meet Poppy Northcutt, the woman who helped bring the Apollo 11 astronauts home safely. *Time*. https://time.com/5614162/apollo-11-anniversary-first-woman/.

[16]National Park Service. (2020). Dr. Chien-Shiung Wu, the first lady of physics. *National Park Service*. https://www.nps.gov/people/dr-chien-shiung-wu-the-first-lady-of-physics.htm.

[17]Dunbar, B. (2019). Jerrie Cobb and the Mercury Project. *National Aeronautics and Space Administration*. nasa.gov/multimedia/imagegallery/image_feature_492.html.

[18]The Editors of Encyclopedia Britannica. (2021). Caroline Herschel. *Encyclopedia Britannica*. britannica.com/biography/Caroline-Lucretia-Herschel.

[19]The Editors of Encyclopedia Britannica. (2021). Ada Lovelace. *Encyclopedia Britannica*. britannica.com/biography/Ada-Lovelace.

[20]The Editors of Encyclopedia Britannica. (2021). Mae Jemison. *Encyclopedia Britannica*. britannica.com/biography/Mae-Jemison.

Acknowledgements

This book would not be possible without the dedicated support of all of the members of my team. Thank you to my mother, my longest-serving advocate and constant supporter and to my father and sister. Thank you to my Girl Scout advisors and the Girl Scout Council of the Nation's Capital for their support of this Gold Award project. Also thank you to my mentors Karen Hickman and Megan Reynolds whose expertise in juvenile books and publishing has been immensely valuable. Of course, this book would have been impossible without the women who shared their stories and advice with me to pass on to my readers; their names can be seen on the "Name Index" page. These inspirational women are on the forefront of their fields and making incredible progress across the space industry. Thank you to Brandi Dean and Shayna Hume for their work, and finally thank you to everyone who proofread this book for their time and advice. This has been a team effort, and the contributions of everyone involved have made this book a reality.

Image Credits

t=top, b=bottom, l=left, r=right
Caltech/MIT/LIGO Laboratory 32tr
DARPA 28tr
Library of Congress 24bl, 28bl
NASA 5l, 6tr, 6bl, 10tr, 11tl, 12bl, 15tl, 18tr, 26tr, 30bl, 34bl, 35tl, 35bl, 37tl, 40bl, 42l
NASA/Ames Research Center/ Daniel Rutter 8tr
NASA/Crew of Expedition 14 40tr
NASA/Johns Hopkins APL/Steve Gribben 30tr
NASA/JPL-Caltech 20tr, 21tl, 22tr, 39tl
NASA/JPL/Cornell University 38tr
NASA/JPL/University of Arizona/ University of Idaho 36tr
NASA/Jet Propulsion Lab-Caltech/SETI Institute 20tr
National Technical Museum "Prof. Dimitrie Leonida", Bucharest 16bl
NOAA Climate.gov 14bl
OAR/National Undersea Research Program (NURP) 24tr
Science Museum Group 38bl
Smithsonian Institution 32bl
U.S. Air Force 34tr
U.S. National Library of Medicine 8bl
U.S. Navy 20bl
USGS 25tl
Wikimedia Commons 10bl, 18bl, 22bl, 36bl

CPSIA information can be obtained
at www.ICGtesting.com
Printed in the USA
BVHW020227050422
633378BV00001B/6